CHESS
FOR
EVERYONE

R. L. BOWLEY

SETTLE PRESS (WIGMORE)

First published by Settle Press (Wigmore)
32 Savile Row
London W1X 1AG

ISBN (Hardback) 0 907070 582
       (Paperback) 0 907070 590

Printed by Villiers Publications Ltd
26a Shepherds Hill, London N6 5AH

CONTENTS

LIST OF ILLUSTRATIONS

FOREWORD

This book has been written for those who have little or no previous knowledge of chess, but who want to learn to play the game well enough to enjoy it. The book is rather more than a set of instructions and rules, and rather less than a manual on the intricacies of play such as opening theory, endplay and the like. Its aim is to be a useful guidebook for chess beginners, short but comprehensive enough to serve as a basis for learning the game.

R. L. Bowley,
Isles of Scilly

I

AN INTRODUCTION TO THE GAME

'Of all the varied amusements which the fertile mind of man has from time to time originated, we know of none which for antiquity, variety, moral excellence and social enjoyment, can in any way be compared with the classic game of chess.' So wrote Howard Staunton, historian and British Chess Champion in the nineteenth century, one of whose greatest services to the game was to give his name to a design of chessmen by Nathaniel Cook, first registered in 1849, which nowadays is universally accepted as standard in all tournament matches. His pieces are of pleasing proportions, easy to identify and pleasant to handle, and it is certainly better for a beginner to buy a Staunton design rather than one of the decorative or elaborate styles suited more for display than play. Larger sets are also preferable to smaller ones because, with the latter, it is easier to overlook piece combinations; many a loser at chess has blamed his defeat on 'not seeing moves his opponent could make'. Sets can be bought in wood or plastic, but those of best quality have chessmen with baize bottoms and are well-weighted – with a good standard of carving on the Knights. Plastic sets of Staunton Chessmen on roll-up boards are what is usual in most chess clubs today.

The game of chess probably originated in India in about the sixth century and was spread by traders to Persia, where Muslim law forbade the carving of images so symbolic shapes came to represent the pieces. The word 'chess' is derived from a Persian word for 'King', and 'checkmate' means 'the King is dead'. Chess then came to Europe, and there is in existence an ivory King from the England of the 12th century, now displayed in the South Wiltshire Museum. In the Middle Ages every Knight was expected to play chess, including Sir Tristan, the hero of medieval romance, who fell in love with Isolde whilst playing the game. In 1474 William Caxton produced *The Game and Playe of The Chesse*, a book complete with woodcut illustrations of games in progress, and the second book ever printed in the English language. However, despite its title, it was not – as this work tries mainly to be – simply a guide to play, but was more a parable for the times in which the chessmen symbolised the different orders or social classes.

In the 16th century (by which time the modern rules had been established) King Philip II of Spain was arranging tournaments, and the game was well known; but chess has never been so popular or so widely played as it is today, when, like tennis, it has a world circuit, growing prize-money and widespread international following.

In the 1920's chess became the national game in the USSR which was the first country to take the game really seriously. It may at first sight seem strange that a game with such obvious elements of a hierarchical order – Kings, Queens and so forth – should be popular in a country striving for classlessness. It may be explained by the belief held by many that the game is of educational value – chess schools exist in Russia to foster young talent – and that its play by workers was likely to help reduce even such abuses as excessive alcoholism.

In practice the educational role of chess is debatable; certainly it encourages close concentration, but many games perform that function. There is little evidence that chess ability is related to other kinds of ability, or even to great intelligence. However, the talent which recognises significant patterns among the pieces does seem to be a requirement of the best chess players, as does an interest in solving problems. Many of the boffins who broke the German Enigma codes during the Second World War were (like Golombek) talented chess players, their work needing great determination and concentration, perhaps the two most important qualities of good chess players

2

after natural talent for the game. This may help to explain why the best chess players tend to be young rather than old, although nobody is likely to equal the infant Cuban prodigy Capablanca, who was beating average adult chess players from the age of four, and was never in time trouble in all his chess career.

At one time chess was seen as an art, but nowadays the competitive element and the prize-money have made it more a sport. There is an element of mental violence in the game, and losing can be very hurtful, with suffering often visible in a chess player's expression. Indeed, chess has been compared to life itself, a constant struggle in which the pain of defeats is compensated by the joy of victories – and few beginners are impervious to the pleasure they experience at their first real win.

But a beginner has basics to master before this can be achieved. First, the distinctive moves of the different pieces must be learnt, and also chess notation; then, a modicum of opening theory needs to be studied, despite the difficulty of coping with the immense amount of work which over the centuries has gone into analysing the opening moves. The fact is that a beginner cannot ignore opening theory altogether, because studying it is part of learning the game, and also because, without some knowledge of the standard openings, a player starts at a disadvantage when facing an opponent who has such knowledge. There are only six different pieces on a board of sixty-four squares, but this allows about 10-to-the-power-of-29 ways of playing the first ten moves. To compete at the highest level requires a deal of arduous preliminary study to become familiar with all the tried variations and theoretical lines of play, and few amateurs have time enough for this; but they can learn the principles of play and, once these are mastered, they should then be able to play up to club standard and enjoy their chess. Moreover, practice at the game is as important a teacher as the study of theory; C. A. Nightingale (chess champion of

Berkshire in the 1960's and 'Birdie' to his pupils at Reading School) used to maintain that the minimum a club player needed of opening theory was a knowledge of one opening set of moves – which he could then always play when drawn White – and two or three defences upon which he could rely when drawn Black. In an article entitled *What is Hard about Chess* in *The Listener* on 8 January 1959, Gerald Abrahamson wrote: '. . . there is very little in the opening (I do not say nothing at all) which absolutely must be learned . . . (but) it helps to be shown a nice analysis in any phase of the game, but only in the way that a poet is helped by reading poetry . . . (and) it is not without interest that some good players (a minority) have had bad memories.'

Of talents a player needs to develop to play chess well, among the most important is the need to 'see ahead' or calculate what is going to happen after the immediate moves have been played. Anyone who has ever watched grandmasters Kasparov and Short in combat over the chess board on television will be aware, from overhearing Kasparov talking to the microphone about the position in front of him, how rapidly a world champion thinks and weighs-up all the possible lines of play.

Also important for a good chess player is being able to distinguish between tactics and strategy. Tactics is dealing with the immediate problems on the board, such as capturing pieces, countering threats of mate, etc. Strategy is the long-term planning, such as castling one's King preparatory to attacking on the other side or positioning a piece on a useful square in preparation for an attack much later in the game. One needs to be a bit of a schemer at chess, not just a person who responds to his opponent's immediate move, but someone with long-term objectives who can 'get up to things'. It is good advice to a beginner not to move quickly – unless, of course, the opponent's move is predictable or obligatory – because the questions: 'Why did my opponent make that last move and what is he aiming to do?' should be in the forefront of one's mind. Often it is essential to see what one's opponent is thinking in order to prepare an adequate response. (An example of a game in which a player becomes pre-occupied with his own attack and oblivious to his opponent's machinations is given at the end of the section on the openings.)

In serious chess the game is played against time limits with two clocks recording the time taken by each player while pondering his moves. If a player must play thirty moves in the first hour (or whatever number of moves and time limit is chosen) then, if he has spent much time moving over the board for his first two dozen moves, he may have to rush the next half-dozen to avoid losing the match through a time penalty. The FIDE tournament rate of play is two hours for each player's first forty moves (as distinct from two-and-a-half hours in world champion-ships), plus one hour for each subsequent set of twenty moves after that (the figure is sixteen in world champion-ships as set by FIDE, which is short for Federation Internationale des Echecs – the world ruling body of chess). Playing to time limits like this helps to ensure that games are not too long and drawn-out; but, if a friendly or ordinary competition game is unfinished when the time set for the whole game has run out, then an adjudication can decide the match – an experienced player being asked to examine the position reached on the board and either declare a draw or one side the winner.

II

CHESS NOTATIONS AND SYMBOLS

There are two principal ways in current use of naming the squares on the board, and it is desirable that a beginner at chess should become familiar with both so as to be able to record his own moves and to follow written ones. In the traditional (or descriptive) notation, the files are known by the names of the pieces which occupy the first rank at the start, and each side views and names the board from its own pieces. In the modern (or short algebraic) notation, the files are lettered a to h and the ranks numbered 1 to 8, as viewed always by the player of the White pieces. Hence under the descriptive notation each square has two names, depending upon whether White or Black pieces are being played; but under the modern system each square has only one name. The pieces are identified by their initial letters, other than the Knight, which, to avoid confusion with the King, is N in the modern system and Kt in traditional notation. The pawn has no identifying symbol in the modern system. From 1981 the International Chess Federation (FIDE) has only recognised the algebraic notation, so in time the traditional descriptive notation may become archaic. Many games in this book are given in both notation, but where only one is used it is short algebraic. Some chess magazines (Pergamon's *Chess*, for example) use symbols for the chess pieces instead of letters, which results in a less tidy presentation, if arguably easier to follow.

BLACK

8	QR8 a8	QKt8 b8	QB8 c8	Q8 d8	K8 e8	KB8 f8	KKt8 g8	KR8 h8
7	QR7 a7	QKt7 b7	QB7 c7	Q7 d7	K7 e7	KB7 f7	KKt7 g7	KR7 h7
6	QR6 a6	QKt6 b6	QB6 c6	Q6 d6	K6 e6	KB6 f6	KKt6 g6	KR6 h6
5	QR5 a5	QKt5 b5	QB5 c5	Q5 d5	K5 e5	KB5 f5	KKt5 g5	KR5 h5
4	QR4 a4	QKt4 b4	QB4 c4	Q4 d4	K4 e4	KB4 f4	KKt4 g4	KR4 h4
3	QR3 a3	QKt3 b3	QB3 c3	Q3 d3	K3 e3	KB3 f3	KKt3 g3	KR3 h3
2	QR2 a2	QKt2 b2	QB2 c2	Q2 d2	K2 e2	KB2 f2	KKt2 g2	KR2 h2
1	QR1 a1	QKt1 b1	QB1 c1	Q1 d1	K1 e1	KB1 f1	KKt1 g1	KR1 h1
	a	b	c	d	e	f	g	h

WHITE

Here is the board in both algebraic and descriptive notations with every square named, but in the descriptive notation it is marked as viewed from the White pieces only.

Abbreviations used in Chess

ch	= check, in descriptive notation
+	= check, in algebraic notation
?	= poor move or weak move
!	= good move or strong move
–	= moves to
x	= captures or takes
ep or ip or en	= en passant (in passing)

0–0	=	castling on the King's side
		(castling short)
0–0–0	=	castling on the Queen's side
		(castling long)
1–0	=	Black resigns
0–1	=	White resigns
mate	=	checkmate, in descriptive notation
+ +	=	checkmate, in algebraic notation
½ v ½	=	draw agreed or forced
dc	=	discovered check
=	=	even game
!!	=	superb move
??	=	a blunder
!?	=	interesting move
?!	=	dubious move

Symbols

♔ = King

♕ = Queen

♖ = Rook

♗ = Bishop

♘ = Knight

No symbol is used for a pawn, the absence of a symbol therefore indicates a pawn move.

III

HOW THE PIECES MOVE

When setting up the pieces, turn the board so that the near right-hand corner square is white. This is very important as the game is not chess if the men are set out with a black square on the right – as they would be for playing draughts. Indeed, it is remarkable how often chessmen can be seen set out incorrectly on boards.

Note that the two sides at chess, though equal, are not identical, in that the White Queen is to the left of the White King, whereas the Black Queen is to the right of her King. Thus the Queens are said to be placed 'on their own colours'. Incidentally, the two sides are called White and Black whether the pieces are coloured yellow and red or yellow and black.

Here is the layout at the start with the pieces shown by means of conventional symbols:

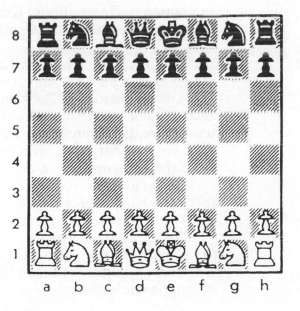

The Starting Positions
It is conventional in chess diagrams to see the board from White's viewpoint, with White's pieces therefore at the bottom of the page and Black's at the top.

A SUMMARY OF THE MOVES

Rook (Castle) – straight lines, up and down files and sideways along ranks.

Bishop – straight lines, up and down the diagonals, keeping to squares of starting colour.

Queen – versatile, like a Rook and a Bishop combined.

King – one square in any direction (except when castling), but never to a square under attack by an opposition piece or adjacent to the opponent's King.

Pawn – always forward, one or two squares on first move, then one square at a time. Takes diagonally. May earn promotion to Queen, Rook, Knight or Bishop if it reaches the eighth rank.

Knight – the only piece which hops and does not go in straight lines. It moves in a fancied combination of Rook and Bishop – one square like a Rook then one square diagonally like a Bishop.

Castling – A player may not castle his King:
(a) if the King or Rook in question have moved;
(b) if the King is in check;
(c) if there is any piece between the Rook and the King;
(d) if the King would have to pass over any square attacked by an opponent's piece.

10

THE MOVES IN MORE DETAIL

The King

Players take it in turn to move, and if they move a piece to a square occupied by an opposing piece, then the opposing piece is taken or captured, i.e. removed from the board. The one exception to this concerns the King, for the sole object of the game of chess is to gain a position in which to take the enemy's King. However, this capture is never actually attained, for the game ends on the move just before this, when there is no way the King can avoid being taken. There is a nice sensitivity here, in that, although the rank and file – and even the Queen – may lay down their lives for their monarch, a player is spared the sight of his King's actual humiliation, when that event finally becomes inevitable. This position is called 'check-mate', whereas, when the King is only threatened with being taken but can move away, it is called 'check'. It is usual (though no longer obligatory) for the player who is threatening on the next move to take his opponent's King to call out 'check'. A King in check either has to move 'out of check' or interpose a piece between himself and the attacking piece, or take the attacking piece either with the King or with some other piece. The King can move in any direction but only one square at a time, so he can take an opposing piece on an adjoining square but not one further away. The King is not allowed to take the piece checking him if by so doing he would still be in check from another opposing piece. However, if the King is a player's only movable piece on the board, and if that King has no move available to him which does not put him in check, this is called 'stalemate', and the game is a draw. Smothered mate is when the King is so hemmed in by pieces that he cannot escape from the check of a Knight – and that is a win for the side with the Knight.

Other ways in which a draw can result and neither player wins are:

11

1. When the game may seem equal and has become boring and both players agree to declare it a draw.
2. When the same position occurs three times (with the same player to move each time), as when a player moves the same piece backwards and forwards; his opponent can claim a draw.
3. When fifty moves have been made without a piece taken or a pawn moved.
4. When there are insufficient forces to secure a mate (e.g. King and two Knights versus a lone King).
5. When a King can be perpetually checked but not mated.

Sometimes the King can be in check by means of 'discovered check', that is where a piece moves away and uncovers an attack on the King's square from another piece. Sometimes the piece moving away also checks the King, and this situation is referred to as 'double check'. But the King is not allowed to move into check, and moving the King out of check is a player's first obligation even if it means losing a piece or indeed the match. One limitation upon the King's movement, which often becomes critical towards the end of the game, is that he may not move so as to be on an adjacent square to the opponent's King – he may not even occupy a square diagonally touching the square occupied by the opponent's King. In the endgame, when the exchange of pieces has reduced each side to perhaps one major piece and a few pawns, this limitation helps the King to become quite a powerful force against the opposing King, combining with his role as an escort to his pawns and their protector against attack from the opposing King and other enemy pieces.

The King has one remarkable and liberating move in conjunction with one of the Rooks, which is usually played near the start of the game and may only be played once in a game. This is 'castling', which means that, provided neither the King nor the Rook in question have yet moved in the game – and intervening squares are not under attack nor the King at that moment in check – then the King

12

moves two squares along the back rank towards the Rook, and the Rook, in the same move, jumps over the King to occupy the square alongside him. Castling is more usual on the King's side of the board (known as castling short), but can also be done on the Queen's side (castling long). The idea is that it removes the King from the centre of the board, where the pawns may have moved away, to the relative security of one side of the board behind a defensive line of three pawns. Castling thus leaves the way open for the pawns on the other side of the board to be advanced in an attack on the enemy position without endangering their King by leaving him exposed and vulnerable. When castling, it is conventional always to move the King first, so that no ambiguity can arise, as when an opponent feels that the player only intended to move the Rook. Indeed, with all moves it is best to observe the rule that a piece touched is a piece played, unless a player just wishes to centre his pieces on their squares, in which case he should inform his opponent by saying 'J'adoube' (I adjust). Asking to take a move back is definitely not de rigueur, and a player is perfectly within his rights to insist that 'once a man has been played, a move has been made'. There is no danger from King Canute, who – as Snorri Sturluson's saga relates – was so annoyed when the Earl he was playing refused to allow him to retract his move, that he had the man executed. However, in friendly games among beginners, it does occasionally seem to make sense to allow an opponent to take back a foolish move which, if made to stand, might spoil a good game and mean that all interest in that particular game was lost. The danger in 'taking back' is doing it so often that it becomes an established practice.

After castling on the King's side, the King is one square from the side of the board (if he castles on the Queen's side he will be two squares from the side of the board). He may appear reassuringly safe behind the three pawns, but there is the danger that the enemy Queen, supported by a Knight or Bishop, may take the King's Knight's pawn (g2) or King's Rook's pawn (h2) and deliver mate; or that, once the protecting Rooks have moved away, an enemy Rook may storm down an empty file and singlehandedly deliver a surprise mate on the back row. Beginners sometimes guard against this eventuality by pushing one of their pawns forward to give the King an escape square, but this could be a waste of a tempo; it may be better to look out for the danger and leave the three pawns undisturbed until such time as there is an additional motive for moving them.

Castling is quite a useful ploy to protect the King and bring one Rook quickly into play, but, if the Queens have been exchanged, it may not be worth wasting a move in this way. Also it is dangerous to castle on a side where the opponent has an open file for his rooks or where his pawns are considerably advanced.

2. AN EMBARRASSING OVERSIGHT (Qxg2)

What every player of the White pieces dreads is overlooking the fact that, although the White King seems to be nestling securely behind a row of protective pawns, the Black Queen can sweep down and capture White's pawn on g2 in front of the King, and – supported by the Bishop – deliver a summary mate.

3. A STORMING ROOK

A Black Rook storming down an empty file and singlehandedly delivering a surprise mate to the White King on his own back row.

The Pawn

Each of a player's eight pawns may move one square forward at a time and never backwards. However, on a pawn's first move it may, if the player so wishes, be moved two squares forward, provided both the squares to be traversed are unoccupied. Unlike other chessmen it cannot move forward to a square occupied by an opposing man; this is because the pawn only captures diagonally, which often results in two pawns being on the same file. This is called 'doubling the pawns', and may prove to be a weakness as the pawns cannot support each other (i.e. one recapture if the other is taken). However, in order that the privilege a pawn enjoys of moving two squares at its first move should not make it possible for the pawn to bypass an opposing pawn coming the other way on an adjoining file, a special rule applies, which was adopted in the time of Ruy Lopez in 16th century Spain. The rule is that the opposing pawn may take the first pawn en passant (in passing), as if it had only moved one square forward; but the option to do this has to be exercised on the very next move or the option lapses. The diagram below illustrates this move:

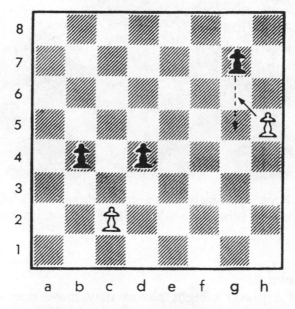

TAKING A PAWN EN PASSANT

If the Black pawn on the g file advances two squares on its first move (g7 to g5), then the White pawn on h5 may take it and move to g6. The reason for this rule is illustrated by the pawn on c2 which otherwise could avoid the two advancing Black pawns by moving to c4. In fact, if White moves c4, then Black takes the pawn either d4 – c3 or b4 – c3.

A pawn is usually considered the humblest or least valuable man on the board, but it possesses great potential. For if a pawn is advanced and reaches the eighth rank, it can be promoted into another man (Q, B, R or N), although usually into a Queen as she is the most useful piece on the board. (If a player already possesses one Queen, an inverted Rook – or a pawn mounted on a Rook – will serve as the second Queen). A backward pawn is one left behind by the advance of its neighbouring pawns, an isolation which is anything but splendid; it makes it vulnerable, and may well lead to its capture.

4. TAKING A PAWN EN PASSANT

Black's King's pawn moves two squares on its first move (e7–e5); White's King's Bishop's pawn (f7) captures it en passant and moves to e6. However, these moves could not be played in this position in a real game because the Black King is already in check from the White Bishop, and so Black is obliged to move his King, interpose a piece or capture the White Bishop. If Black has no piece with which to take the offending Bishop, then probably his best move in this position is to play K-R1 (Kh8) to avoid a long-term threat from the White Bishop. Alternatively, he could play pawn to K3 (e6) – though not to K4 (e5) – and this 'gets the Black King out of check'.

5. THE KNIGHT'S MOVES

Spoilt for choice: the central Knight has eight men he can
choose to capture.

The Knight
The Knight is the only piece which may jump over the
other pieces (other than a Rook when castling). It moves
two squares along a file or rank, and then one square to the
left or the right. Alternatively, it can be thought of as
moving one square along a file or rank and then two
squares to the left or right – it amounts to the same thing. A
Knight in the middle of the board thus has a choice of eight
squares to which to move, provided each of these squares is
not occupied by one of the pieces of his own side. A Knight
on the side ranks or files has a choice of only four squares to
go to (and only two squares when in a corner), so for that
reason it is regarded as better for the Knights normally to
try to avoid moving to the edges. A Knight is usually

18

valued as nearly equal to a Bishop – depending on the general position of the pieces – so an exchange with a Bishop is often a fair swop, particularly if it improves the position. But neither a Bishop nor a Knight are worth exchanging for a Rook except in most exceptional circumstances, and it would usually take the capture of at least three pawns to justify losing a Knight or a Bishop.

It is worth stressing that the position of pieces counts for almost everything when valuing the pieces, but if this factor is temporarily discounted, then it is possible to compare their relative values. Howard Staunton did this in his *Chess Player's Handbook* of 1847, using rather over precise arithmetical estimations as follows:

Chessman		Value	Squares Covered
pawn	=	1.00	2
Knight	=	3.05	8
Bishop	=	3.50	13
Rook	=	5.48	14
Queen	=	9.94	27
King	=	invaluable, of course	8

This makes a Knight worth more than three pawns, and two Bishops worth more than a Bishop and a Knight; but a Bishop and two pawns are only just ahead of a Rook. The state of the game as well as the position has an effect on valuations; a Queen in the middle of the game, when there are still plenty of pieces on the board, is possibly worth two Rooks and a pawn; but in the endgame she is hardly as valuable as two Rooks.

6. AN INSPIRED HOP

On all sides the Black King is protected . . . but, too much!
A leaping Knight finds the Black King smothered, and delivers
mate in one inspired hop.

The Knight's move
The leaping Knight is a tricky piece with a strange manner
of moving, and one of its dangerous moves is when it forks
opposing pieces, i.e. threatens the squares of two pieces
simultaneously, so that, although one of them may move
out of danger, the other is taken. Pieces other than the
Knight can also carry out a fork, but a Knight's fork is
often harder to foresee. One point to notice about the
Knight is that its curious move is sometimes a disadvantage,
for it can take the Knight some time to reach a particular
square; it will take it four moves to cross over the whole
board, and to move just two squares away along a diagonal
(f3 to c5 for example) would take it no less than four moves.

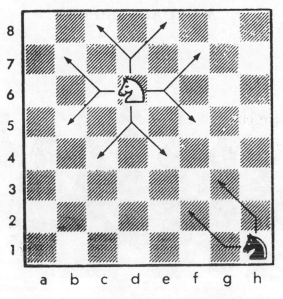

This limitation upon the Knight can be exploited (particularly by an opponent trying to queen pawns).

The Rook
The Rook (or Castle as it is sometimes called by non-chess players) moves like a plus sign up the files or across the ranks. It rarely sees much of the action at the opening of the game, but becomes important in the middle and endgame, and is second to the Queen in value.

The Bishop
The Bishop moves along the diagonal for as many squares as a player desires, provided there are no other pieces in the way. One Bishop travels on the white squares and the other on the black, so they never meet.

7.   MUTUAL SUPPORT

White's Bishop and pawn are giving each other mutual support, while the Bishop is threatening f7, the square occupied by Black's weakest pawn.

The Queen
The Queen can move like a Bishop or a Rook, which makes her the most valuable piece. (After her King, of course, whose safety is beyond computation.)

It should be noted that traditionally all the chessmen are called men, while *pieces* are all the men which are not pawns. The pieces are divided into major pieces (Queens and Rooks) and minor pieces (Bishops and Knights). However, beginners (and others) tend to refer loosely to all men as pieces, and the distinction can become blurred. Moreover, because of modern objections to the use of such words as 'chairman' and 'mankind' owing to their perceived sexist connotations – and remembering that in chess even

22

the Queen is called a man – if all chessmen are referred to as pieces, this meets the objection, avoids giving offence, and is without real harm to the game.

However, the rules of chess are strict about some matters. If an illegal move has been made without either player noticing and pointing it out – as sometimes happens for instance when a beginner moves a piece only to realise that his King was already in check – then the rule is that the men should be set out in the positions they occupied before the illegal move took place, and the game re-started. If it is possible, the offending player should play the man with which he made the illegal move, but this may not be possible when the illegality was an unrecognised check, since it may be that only moving the King will constitute a legal move. Thus the penalty of having to move the offending piece cannot in this case be enforced, and the rules provide that no alternative penalty should be exacted.

The rules also make it clear that a move is not completed until a player has taken away his hand from his man; however, as soon as he has touched one of his men, he must move it somewhere   though he may change his mind in mid air as to the square upon which he wishes it to alight.

The rules do forbid players or spectators from commenting upon moves while a game is in progress, but, of course, this need not unduly inhibit beginners who may wish to profit from advice from onlookers, provided it is evenly given and helps the beginners to learn the game.

Two terms sometimes encountered in chess are the skewer and the sandwich. The skewer is a move rather similar to a fork, but involving a Bishop or Queen threatening a number of opposing pieces on squares along a diagonal. In the following, contrived position, Black's Queen's Bishop has White's two Rooks and White's two Knights in his sights along the line of the diagonal, and three of these White pieces are en prise (unprotected). [What White is doing bringing his Rook into the centre of the board so early in the game is another matter.]

23

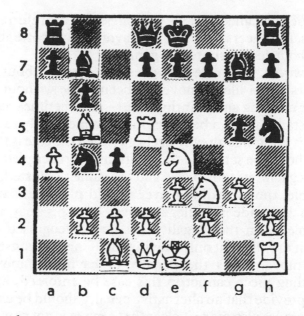

The skewer can also involve a Rook or Queen in an attack on two or more pieces on the same file or rank, such that the piece nearest the attacker is compelled to move, leaving the other piece to be taken. For example, imagine Black's Queen on e8 and Black's King on e5, then, if White moves a Rook to e1, it will check the Black King and oblige him to move, so exposing the Black Queen to capture by the Rook.

A sandwich move is one made in between other move developments, as when, for example, a threatened enemy piece, which is without chance of rescue, is left to be captured at the subsequent move.

8. THE PIN

The White Knight is pinned by the Black Bishop. If the White Knight moves, the Black Bishop can capture the White Queen.

The Black Knight is pinned. It cannot move because this would disclose check on the Black King from the White Bishop. However if Black interposes his Bishop between his Knight and his King, then the Knight is released from the pin.

IV

THE OPENINGS: OBJECTIVES AND MOVES

Players begin the game by choosing a colour. This is important as the rule is that White always has the first move, and there is a small initial advantage in this – a gain of a tempo. An exception to this rule occurred in 1809 when Napoleon played Maelzel's automaton, a machine secretely containing a small chess player – originally a man who had lost both legs – and insisted on being Black and on having the first move; but, then, Napoleon always cheated – even when playing patience by himself.

Having the first move also enables White to choose the opening he wishes to play, and Black is at first on the defensive. One way of choosing colours is for one player to hold a pawn hidden in his hand, with a pawn of the other colour hidden in his other hand, and to ask his opponent to choose one of his hands – a more distinguished procedure than the ubiquitous tossing of a coin. Players then move their own pieces alternately, but they may not make two moves consecutively nor are they allowed to pass and make no move at all.

The major consideration of each player at the start of the game is to develop some pieces, i.e. bring them into play. Moving either the King's pawn (e2) or the Queen's pawn (d2) will allow the Bishops eventually to emerge from behind the pawns, while the Knights can always jump over the pawns. By contrast, moving a Rook's pawn (a2 or h2) does not allow any major piece to develop other than the Rook, and so is not recommended as an early move.

Another objective at the start of the game is to try to exercise some control of the centre of the board, for centrally-placed pieces can exercise influence over all areas of the board. This does not necessarily mean occupying the four centre squares with one's own pieces, but positioning pieces so that they could occupy those squares, if it became

26

desirable. For example, the Bishop has an alternative development by advancing the King's Knight's pawn one square (g2–g3) or alternatively, advancing the Queen's Knight's pawn one square (b2–b3) and placing the Bishop in its place (g2 or b2). This is called fianchettoing, and places the Bishop in a useful position on the flank (which might be described as making it equivalent to long-range artillery), and from here the Bishop can help control the centre of the board.

A further objective at the start of the game is to gain tempi (timing). For this reason it is better not to move a piece more than once in the first few moves of the game – unless forced to do so, of course – because of the danger of losing tempi and allowing one's opponent's pieces to take up useful positions while most of one's own are still stuck in their starting places behind the pawns. For instance, if the Queen is brought out early, she is liable to be chased around the board by one's opponent, who thereby gains tempi and develops his pieces, while one's own moves are wasted in defending the Queen. If, on the other hand, one's opponent's Queen is out on the board and is menacing one's position, then the most effective piece to counter her is one's own Queen; in these circumstances the Queen may be developed from her starting square however early in the game it is. But it is almost always a mistake at the start of the game to assault the enemy position with only one piece; a combination of men, including pawns, is usually more likely to bring success. Generally, it is unwise to leave a man en prise – that is in a position where it is under threat of being taken – unless it is adequately supported by enough men to retake it or to take an equivalent enemy man on another square.

9. DANISH GAMBIT

The Danish Gambit. White is three pawns down at this stage of the game after Black's 4th move, but is about to win one pawn back when the White Bishop captures Black's bold pawn on b2. White has gained tempi for the loss of two pawns – but look how powerfully placed are his Bishops.

In order to gain tempi (the plural of tempo) it is sometimes worth even the sacrifice of men. **The Danish Opening** does this, although it may seem rather a rash waste of material. [Both descriptive and algebraic notations have been used for the moves of some of these openings to familiarise the beginner with their use.]

	White		*Black*	
1.	P – K4	(e4)	P – K4	(e5)
2.	P – Q4	(d4)	P × P	(e×d4)
3.	P – QB3	(c3)	P × P	(d×c3)
4.	B – QB4	(Bc4)	P × P	(c×b2)

28

White has sacrificed three pawns to date

5.   QB × P   (B×b2)   P – Q4   (d5)

here one pawn is gained back and both Bishops have been developed, while Black has little development.

The game could continue in the following way:

6. B × QP   (B×d5)   Kt – KB3 (Nf6)
7. B × Pch (B×f7+)   K × B   (K×f7)
8. Q × Q   (Q×d8)   B – Kt5ch (Bb4+)
9. Q – Q2   (Qd2)   B × Qch (B×d2+)
10. Kt × B   (N×d2)   P – B4   (c5)

Thus material exchanges have been equal and both sides have a passed pawn (which is a pawn which has no opposing pawn either on its file or on adjoining files to frustrate its progress to promotion on the eighth rank).
    The immediate line of play from move 10 is likely to consist of both sides developing their pieces and each trying to defend his own passed pawn and attack his opponent's passed pawn. The White King still has the option of castling, but the Black King cannot; however, Black can obtain the same position as castling would have have given him by bringing his Rook into play on K1 (e8) – so bearing another piece on to the White pawn on K4 (c4) – and moving the King to KKt1 (g8). But, as the Queens have been exchanged, Black may consider it more important to develop his pieces than to castle his King.
    The Danish opening is not often played, but the following openings are selected from many which are commonly played. They have been chosen because a beginner can learn many of the important principles of the game by following them through on a board.

(1). **Guicco Piano** (Italian for 'quiet game')

White		Black	
1.	P – K4 (e4)	P – K4	(e5)
2.	Kt – KB3 (Nf3)	Kt – QB3	(Nc6)

Because White always has the first move in chess, White usually takes the offensive initially and Black the defensive. Here White is attacking Black's advanced pawn with the Knight, and Black is defending it with his Knight.

3.	B – B4	(Bc4)	B – B4	(Bc5)

Both bishops are brought out to threaten the square holding their opponent's weakest pawn – King's Bishop's pawn (f2 and f7).

4.	P – Q3	(d3)	P – Q3	(d6)

White should avoid playing P – QR3 (a2). If the Bishop wastes time checking White's King, it simply gives White an opportunity to develop his pieces.

5.	B – K3	(Be3)	B – Kt3	(Bb6)
6.	Kt – B3	(Nc3)	Kt – B3	(Nf6)
7.	Kt – K2	(Ne2)	B – K3	(Be6)
8.	B – Kt3	(Bb3)	Kt – K2	(Ne7)
9.	castles	(0 – 0)	castles	(0 – 0)

an even position.

Another possible line of development in this opening is:

White		Black	
4.	P – QB3 (c3)	Kt – KB3	(Nf6)

White is preparing an attack in the centre, while Black

30

brings another piece into action – attacking the King's pawn (e4)

5.	P – Q4	(d4)	P × P	(e×d4)
6.	P × P	(c×d4)	B–QKt5 ch	(Bb4+)

and the game continues.

10. GUICCO PIANO

Guicco Piano: all is set for a quiet if, as yet, stodgy game by two unhurried players intent on development. Both have castled short and have all their minor pieces in play.

11. FACING TWO KNIGHTS

A quiet development against a Two Knight's Defence by Black; but what happens if White should play Ng5 (threatening N×f7 forking Queen and Rook)? If Black plays d5, this deals with the immediate danger; but, after e×d5, Na5 is sound – followed later perhaps by N×d5.

Here is how two beginners might play this game, with White determined to assault the f pawn.

1.	e4	e5
2.	Nf3	Nc6
3.	Bc4	Nf6
4.	Ng5	d5
5.	e×d5	N×d5?

A better move for Black would have been Na5 threatening the Bishop

| 6. | Qh5 | looks rather too bold a move |

6. . . .   g6
7. N×f7. If Black now takes White's Queen, then
    White will take Black's Queen, capture the Knight,
    be a pawn up and have messed up Black's defences,
    leaving Black with an unsupported e pawn
7. . . .   K×f7
8. Qf3+ threatening to win back the Knight

Here is another offshoot of this development which it is
worthwhile a beginner studying, for a Two Knight's
Defence is often to be faced, and some knowledge of these
moves could give a beginner the edge over an opponent:

	White	*Black*
1.	e4	e5
2.	Nf3	Nc6
3.	Bc4	Nf6
4.	Ng5	d5
5.	e×d5	N×d5

the temptation for Black to recapture immediately is very
strong.

6. 0 – 0   Be7
    If Black plays Q×g5, then White can play B×d5.
7. N×f7   K×f7
    White is sacrificing a Knight for a pawn in order to
    drive the Black King into the middle of the board
    where he will be more vulnerable.
8. Qf3+   Ke6
    To retain his material advantage, Black moves his
    King to protect his Knight on d5 now under attack
    from Bishop and Queen.
9. Nc3   Ncb4
    White brings another piece to attack the Black
    Knight pinned on d5, and Black supports his

Knight with the other Knight.

[At this point a variety of different moves by White are possible including a3 and d4].

10. d4   c6

Black has the c pawn defending the pinned Knight for when the other Knight on b4 is driven away; but alternative moves for Black are Rf8 (attacking White's Queen) or b5 to move White's Bishop.

11. Qe4   Bd6

Black is defending his e pawn. Bf6 would have served the same purpose, except that Black is probably keeping the f file free for his Rook to command it later from f8.

12. a3   Qa5
13. Rb2   Na6

Black has to retreat the Knight to a relatively useless position on the sidelines.

14. b4   Qb6

The Black Queen has to retire, but is loath to move to c7, which looks a promising square for the Knight at present on a6.

15. B×d5   c×d5
16. Qg4+   Kf7
17. Qf3+   Kg6

If Black retreats his King to g8, not only is the Rook blocked in but Q×d5 prolongs the problem and loses a pawn.

18. Qg3+   Kf7
19. d×e5   Bb8
20. Qf3+   Kg8

and an interesting game continues.

By contrast, here is a game played over a century ago which is illustrative of the Two Knights' Defence:

White	*Black*
(Mr Anderssen)	(Mr De Rivière)

1.	e4	e5
2.	Nf3	Nc6
3.	Bc4	Nf6
4.	Ng5	d5
5.	e×d5	Na5
6.	Bb5+	c6
7.	d×c6	b×c6
8.	Be2; this seems a sensible move, although Staunton says of it that after this move: 'White must get a bad game'.	
8.	. . .	h6
9.	Nf3	e4 White is certainly on the retreat but is a pawn up.
10.	Ne5	Qd4
11.	f4	the White Knight must be defended or moved and Anderssen said this move was better than Ng4.
11.	. . .	Bc5; Black is now mounting a formidable counter attack and threatening mate by Qf2.
12.	Rf1	Qd6
13.	C3	Nb7
14.	b4	Bb6
15.	Na3	0–0
16.	Nc4	Qc7
17.	a4	a6
18.	N×b6	Q×b6
19.	a5	Qc7
20.	Kf2	

this is a deep manoeuvre which at first sight looks like a mistake.

20.	. . .	Nd5
21.	Kg1	N×f4
22.	R×f4	Q×e5
23.	Qf1	Nd6
24.	Ba3	f5
25.	Rd1	g5
26.	Rf2	Ra7
27.	Bc4+	N×c4
28.	Q×c4+	Qe6
29.	Q×e6+	B×e6
30.	b5	a×b5
31.	B×f8	K×f8
32.	Ra1	Ke7
33.	Re2	h5
34.	h4	g×h4
35.	Kh2	Kf6
36.	Ra3	Bc4
37.	Re1	Bd3
38.	Kg1	Kg5
39.	Kf2	Kg4
40.	Rh1	Bc2
41.	Ke3	Ba4
42.	R(a)a1	R×a5
43.	R×h4+	Kg5

If the Black King takes the Rook, then White plays Kf4 and, although Black can stall the inevitable by sacrificing Bishop and Rook, when White plays Rh1 it is mate.

44.	Rh1; now White's two Rooks are in tandem (supporting one another) and begin to show their power over Black's Rook and Bishop.	
44.	. . .	Bb3
45.	R×h5+	Kf6

46.	Kf4	Be6
47.	Rh7	Bf7
48.	Rh6+	Bg6
49.	Rd7	e3
50.	K×e3	Kg5

and White went on to win the game.

(2). The **Evans Gambit** is an offshoot from the Guicco Piano and was first played in a tournament in 1826 by W. D. Evans:

	White		*Black*	
1.	P – K4	(e4)	P – K4	(e5)
2.	Kt – KB3	(Nf3)	Kt – QB3	(Nc6)
3.	B – B4	(Bc4)	B – B4	(Bc5)
4.	P – Qkt4	(b4)	B × Ktp	(B×b4)

Here White is sacrificing a pawn in order to achieve a positional advantage. Black's best move is probably to take the pawn.

5.	P – B3	(c3)	B – QR4	(Ba5)

If the Bishop moves backwards on the other diagonal, Black's game is somewhat cramped.

6.	castles	(0 – 0)	P – Q3	(d6)
7.	P – Q4	(d4)	B – Kt3	(Bb6)

This last move of Black's was played by Lasker in a tournament in 1898 and recommended by him 'to convert Black's extra material into positional advantage'. But there are many other lines of play. The game might continue:

8.	P × P	(d×e5)	P × P	(d×e5)

9.	Q × Qch	(Q×d8+)	Kt × Q	(N×d8)
10.	Kt × P	(N×e5)		

and Black has the better pawn position, but is no longer a pawn up. White's pawn on QB3 (c3) has no supporting pawns on either file beside it (b file and d file), and the QR pawn (a2) is also isolated, so both are weak.

However the Evans Gambit may be declined, in which case the game could proceed in the following way:

4.	P – QKt4	(b4)	B – Kt3	(Bb6)
5.	P – Kt5	(b5)	Kt – R4	(Na5)
6.	Kt × P	(N×e5)	Kt – R3	(Nh6)
7.	P – Q4	(d4)	P – Q3	(d6)
8.	B × Kt	(B×h6)	P × B	(g×h6)

12. THE EVANS GAMBIT

The Evans Gambit accepted.

9. Kt × P   (N×f7)   Q – B3   (Qe7)

White's Knight is forking Queen and Rook

10. Kt × R   (N×h8)   B × P   (B×d4)

Black's Bishop is now forking the Knight and the Rook.

11. Q – R5ch (Qh5+)   K – K2   (Kd7)

At this point White is a Rook and a Pawn up, but so many of his pieces are insecure that the material advantage may only be temporary.

(3). The **Ruy Lopez**

An opening attack by White named after Ruy Lopez, a 16th century priest at the court of King Philip II and Spain's ablest player, whom the King is said to have made a bishop (of Segovia) in recognition of his skill at chess. There are many lines of defence; here is one:

	White		*Black*	
1	P – K4	(e4)	P – K4	(e5)
2.	Kt – KB3	(Nf3)	Kt – QB3	(Nc6)
3.	B – Kt5	(Bb5)	. . .	

Here is the divergence from the Giucco Piano. Instead of the move to QB4 (c4) threatening KB pawn (f7), the Bishop moves to attack the Knight. In the event of Black's Queen's pawn (d7) moving out to release the Bishop, the Black Knight will be pinned (i.e. not able to move because that will open check on the King).

13. RUY LOPEZ

Ruy Lopez: in the position above White has to make his 4th move. This is Ba4, which removes the immediate threat to the Bishop from the Black pawn on a6 while maintaining the potential pin on the Black Knight for when eventually Black advances his d pawn.

3.	. . .		P – QR3	(a6)
4.	B – QR4	(Ba4)	. . .	

this maintains the threat

4.	. . .		Kt – KB3	(Nf6)
5.	castles	(0 – 0)	. . .	

If Black now takes White's pawn which is en prise, White

can regain the pawn by the following play:

5.	...		Kt × P	(N×e4)
6.	R – K1	(Re1)	P – KB4	(f5)
7.	P – Q3	(d3)	Kt – KB3	(Nf6)
8.	B × Kt	(B×c6)	QP × B	(dxc6)
9.	Kt × P	(n×e5)	...	

and White has the added advantage of a Rook on an open file against the Black King. For the purpose of demonstration let us suppose that Black now fails to play his Bishop to Q2 (Bd7) but, in a moment of aberration, plays the disastrous move B – Q3 (Bd6). Then the White Knight can take the Black pawn (C6) thus opening check on the Black King from the Rook on e1. This is called 'discovered check'. Black cannot take the Knight with the Bishop because he has either to move out of check or interpose a piece, and whichever he chooses, Black's Queen is taken by the Knight – and Black should resign.

Instead of Black taking White's pawn on move 5, it might be more prudent for him to play a development move:

5.	...		B – K2	(Be7)
6.	R – K1	(Re1)	P – QKt4	(b5)
7.	B – QKt3	(Bb3)	castles	(0 – 0)

Both sides have now castled and are preparing to develop their major pieces. White has lost some tempi by moving his Bishop three times, but it has ended up in a strong position. There are, of course, many variations in this opening after move 4.

A trap to play (or to avoid) comes in the Ruy Lopez Opening as follows:

1.	e4	e5

2.	Nf3		Nc6
3.	Bf5		a6
4.	Ba4		Nf6
5.	Nc3		d6
6.	d4		b5
7.	Bb3		e×d4

this last move of White's seems a natural move, but is in fact a mistake; a better move would have been d×e5 countering Black's threat to the Bishop by attacking Black's Knight.

| 8. | N×d4 | | N×d4 |

White must take the pawn otherwise he just loses a pawn for nothing.

| 9. | Q×d4 | | c5 |

Now White's Queen is under attack, and, wherever she goes seeking a place of safety, Black continues to advance his c pawn winning the White Bishop at the next move.

(4).   The **Vienna Gambit**

1.	P – K4	(e4)	P – K4	(e5)
2.	Kt – QB3	(Nc3)	Kt – KB3	(Nf6)
3.	P – KB4	(f4)	P – Q4	(d5)

which leads to an open game.

(5).   The **Queen's Gambit** – in which Queen's Bishop's pawn is sacrificed.

| 1. | P – Q4 | (d4) | P – Q4 | (d5) |
| 2. | P – QB4 | (c4) | P × P | (d×c4) |

White temporarily sacrifices a pawn to gain some control of the centre. (Black should not try too hard to hold on to that advanced pawn – it is too far ahead and on its own at too early a stage in the game).

42

(6). The **King's Gambit** – in which King's Bishop's pawn is sacrificed.

1. P – K4   (e4)   P – K4   (e5)
2. P – KB4   (b4)

This opens up the King's Bishop's file and can lead to a strenuous game.

14. THE KING'S GAMBIT

The King's Gambit is so-called because White is offering the King's Bishop's pawn to be taken in the hope that by this sacrifice he can break open the f file and launch a massive attack. Until this century it was usual for Black to accept gambits (i.e. take the men offered) and try to retain the material advantages so gained; but this sometimes led Black into difficulties, so increasingly in this century gambits came to be declined (i.e. the proffered men were not taken). Modern-day analysis tends to suggest that the best response to most gambits – other than the Queen's Gambit – may be to accept them (i.c. to take the men offered), but then not to strive too hard to retain the material advantage gained but concentrate instead on development.

(7). The **English Opening**

The English opening is so called because it was an Englishman, Howard Staunton, who first tried it in a championship match in 1843, taking his French opponent completely by surprise by starting the game with such an unorthodox move.

White		*Black*	
1.	P – QB4 (c4)	P – K4	(e5)
2.	Kt – QB3 (Nc3)	Kt – QB3	(Nc6)

and pieces are developed.

(8). The **King's Pawn Counter-Gambit**

A little-played gambit concerning the King's pawn is fun to play when one has an opponent of modest ability known to be rash and impetuous on the board.

White		*Black*	
1.	P – K4 (e4)	P – K4	(e5)
2.	Kt – KB3 (Nf3)	Kt – QB3	(Nc6)
3.	B – QB4 (Bc4)	Kt – Q5	(Nd4)?

This move is not theoretically a sound one, for it advances a minor piece too far, too early, before other pieces are developed; but Black is counting upon White being tempted by the proffered pawn and unfamiliar with the move.

4.   Kt × P   (N×e5)   . . .

It may seem to a beginner playing White that at this point he has the makings of a promising attack: Black's King's Bishop's pawn (f7) is under threat of capture from the White Knight (which, if it took the pawn, would then be forking the Rook and the Queen) and from the Bishop, which, if it took the pawn, would administer a check to the Black King forcing him to move and denying him the option of castling.

4.   . . .   Q – KKt4 (Qg5)

At a cursory glance this move of Black's may not seem to alter the situation or counter White's attack. White may now feel committed to his line of play and be blind to Black's counter-schemes. After all, if the White Knight takes the King's Bishop's pawn (f7), he will still be forking the Rook and the Queen.

5.   Kt × KBP (N×f7)   Q × KKtP (Q×g2)
    [a better move is B × f7+]

Now the danger of Black's counter-attack may begin to dawn upon the hasty White player. Black is almost threatening mate on the next move by taking the Rook with his Queen. White could play d3 or Nc3, but loses the Rook if he does. There is one defensive move for White:

6.   R – KB1   (Rf1)   Q × KPch   (Q×e4+)
7.   B – K2   (Be2)   . . .

If White plays Q – K2 (Qe2), Black takes the Queen with the Knight and, if the White Bishop recaptures, wins the other Knight also.

7.   . . .   Kt × QBPch (N×c2+)
8.   Q × Kt   (Q×c2)   Q × Q   (Q×c2)

And now both White's Bishops are en prise, and White should resign so as not to prolong the agony any further.

But the game might, of course, be played quite differently

45

after the 4th move:

	White	*Black*
1.	e4	e5
2.	Nf3	Nc6
3.	Bc4	Nd4
4.	N × e5	Qg5
5.	B × f7+	Ke7
6.	Nc3 is a better move than d3. If the Black Queen takes the Knight on e5, she suffers the indignity of being chased about the board, starting with f4. Note that the Queen cannot take White's pawn on f4 because Nd5 would fork the Black Queen and King.	
6.	. . .	Q × g2
7.	Rf1	Nf6

The game could then progress into all sorts of complications.

V

DEFENCES

Some conventional defences have already been indicated in the above openings, but one common one is **The Sicilian**:

	White		Black	
1.	P – K4	(e4)	P – QB4	(c5)
2.	Kt – KB3	(Nf3)	P – Q3	(d6)
3.	P – Q4	(d4)	P × P	(c×d4)
4.	Kt × P	(N×d4)	Kt – KB3	(Nf6)
5.	QKt – QB3	(Nc3)	P – KKt3	(g6)

Black now plans to fianchetto his Bishop and, with two White Knights, a pawn and a Rook on the diagonal in the line of its fire, there may be opportunities to capture one of them later in the game. In such ways does the Sicilian Defence give Black opportunities to counter-attack.

Here is an example of a game in which Black used the Sicilian Defence:

1.	e4	c5
2.	Nf3	d6
		(Nc6 is also popular)
3.	d4	c×d4
4.	N×d4	Nf6

Black's idea is to attack White's pawn while developing a piece.

5.	Nc3	a6

White's plan is to defend the pawn while developing a piece, and Black anticipates a move by the White Knight to b5 which can be forestalled by a6.

6. Bg5   e6

White develops his Bishop which will pin the Black Knight on f6 if Black moves his e pawn – which he does.

7. f4   Be7

White starts an attack, while Black releases the pin.

8. Qf3   Qc7

9. O–O–O   Nbd7

Note that when two similar pieces – in this instance the two Knights – can move to the same square, the second letter denotes the file of the Knight so that there will be no confusion as to which Knight has moved.

10. Bd3   h6

Black is trying to induce White's Bishop to retreat to the side of the board, but White has an answer.

11. Qh3   Nb6

If Black had played h×g5, White could then play Q×h8+. Instead, Black plays a move which will open up the White Queen to attack from the Bishop when Black's e pawn advances.

12. f5   e5

White covers the line of attack on his Queen and keeps up the momentum of his attack.

13. Nde2   Bd7

Again it is necessary in the notation to specify which Knight has moved to e2 by indicating that it is the one on the d file. Black meanwhile develops his Bishop.

14. Kb1   Bc6

White recognises the vulnerability of his a pawn and moves his King to protect it, while Black attacks White's backward pawn on e4, which has no friendly pawns on either adjacent files to protect it. Knight and Bishop are doing their best to protect it, but White's e pawn has become the focus of attack and defence.

| 15. | Be3 | Nbd7 |
| 16. | g4 | o–o–o |

White's attack continues on the King's side now that he has castled long; Black responds by castling long to avoid White's advancing pawns.

| 17. | Qf3 | f5 |

and the game continued.

Another popular defence is the **French Defence**:

	White		*Black*	
1.	P – K4	(e4)	P – K3	(e6)
2.	P – Q4	(d4)	P – Q4	(d5)

White should not now play P – KB3 (f3) in defence of his King's pawn (e4) or he may lose a pawn and a Rook, but he could take the pawn, or push forward with his King's pawn (e5), or defend the King's pawn (e4) with his Queen's Knight (c3).

The **Nimzo-Indian Defence** involves the pin of a White Knight:

1.	P – Q4	(d4)	Kt – KB3	(Nf6)
2.	P – K4	(c4)	P – K3	(e6)
3.	Kt – QB3	(Nc3)	B – QKt5	(Bb4)

Black now has the opportunity to 'double' White's pawns by taking the Knight, and doubled pawns are weaker because they cannot support each other. If White does not bring out his Queen's Knight, but plays:

3.	Kt – KB3	(Nf3)	P – QKt3	(b6)

this is called the Queen's Indian Defence and enables Black to fianchetto his Bishop.

The **King's Indian Defence** is one of the most popular defences against the Queen's pawn opening, and play often goes like this:

	White		*Black*	
1.	P – Q4	(d4)	Kt – KB3	(Nf6)
2.	P – QB4	(c4)	P – KKt3	(g6)
3.	Kt – QB3	(Nc3)	B – KKt2	(Bg7)
4.	P – K4	(e4)	P – Q3	(d6)
5.	P – KB3	(f3)	castles	(0 – 0)
6.	B – K3	(Be3)	P – K4	(e5)
7.	P – Q5	(d5)		

Black is well entrenched but his Bishops look a little frustrated.

The **Old Indian** is another variation:

	White		*Black*	
1.	P – Q4	(d4)	Kt – KB3	(Nf6)
2.	P – QB4	(c4)	P – Q3	(d6)
3.	Kt – QB3	(Nc3)	P – K4	(e5)

Philidor's Defence is as follows:

	White		*Black*	
1.	P – K4	(e4)	P – K4	(e5)
2.	Kt – KB3	(Nf6)	P – Q3	(d6)

Other well-used openings after White's first move of e4 include: **Petroff's Defence**: 1. e4 e5 2. Nf3 Nf6; the **Scotch Opening**: 1. e4 e5 2. Nf3 Nc6 3. d4; the **Creco Counter Gambit**: 1. e4 e5 2. Nf3 f5; and **Alekhine's Defence**: e4 Nf6. If White's first move is d4, then there are: the **Slav Defence**: 1. d4 d5 2. c4 c6; the **Albin**

Counter Gambit: 1. d4 d5 2. c4 e5 – but which loses Black a pawn early in the game; the **Dutch Defence**: 1. d4 f5; and the **Tarrasch Opening**: 1. d4 d5 2. c4 e6 3. Nc3 c5 – all of which beginners may like to experiment with against each other to provide variety. On the whole, however, beginners are advised to stick to openings where they feel more confident; one of the fascinations of chess is the immense amount of varied play which is possible from even the stock openings.

15. SHORT-CASTLED AND BISHOP FIANCHETTOED

The Black King is short-castled and the King's Bishop is fianchettoed – a strong defence.

A fashionable defence in the 1980's – partly perhaps because Karpov and Kasparov are both fond of it – is the

Grünfeld Defence. The opening moves follow the English Opening and are worth a beginner following them through to see how grandmasters develop their pieces. Here is the defence in short algebraic notation:

1.	c4	c5
2.	Nf3	Nf6
3.	Nc3	d5
4.	c×d5	N×d5
5.	d4	N×c3
6.	b×c3	g6
7.	e3	Bg7
8.	Bd3	0 – 0
9.	0 – 0	Qc7
10.	Rb1	b6
11.	Qe2	Rd8

and both sides are poised for attack, the centre of the board being the focus of attention.

The **Caro Kann Defence** is also much played:

1.	e4	c6
2.	d4	d5
3.	Nd2	d×e4
4.	N×e4	Nd7
5.	Nf3	Ngf6
6.	N×f6+	N×f6
7.	c3	Bg4 (pinning the White Knight)
8.	h3	B×f3 (or Black could play Bh5 maintaining the pin)
9.	Q×f3	e6
10.	Bc4	Be7
11.	0 – 0	N – d5
12.	Be3	Q – b6

and both sides have pieces developed, though Black must soon find time to castle his King. Notice how again the centre of the board is the focus of the action.

In defence Black has to be careful to develop his pieces and not to allow White to mount too much attack on f7. Consider the following disastrous game for Black, which is a foregone conclusion as soon as Black has made his 5th move!

1.	e4	e5
2.	Nf3	Nf6
3.	Bc4	N×e4 (the chance of being a pawn up is too tempting for Black)
4.	Nc3	Nc5
5.	N×e5	f6?? (White can now announce mate in 8!)
6.	Qh5+	g6
7.	Bf7+	Ke7
8.	Nd5+	Kd6
9.	Nc4+	Kc6
10.	Nb4+	Kb5
11.	a4+	K×Nb4
12.	c3+	Kb3
13.	Qd1++	

a remarkable testimony to the power of Knights, and to the vulnerability of the King once driven out from behind his protecting pawns in the early phases of the game.

Sometimes opening moves display a remarkable symmetry, as in the following game where Black adopts almost copycat tactics.

	White	Black
1.	e4	e5
2.	Nf3	Nc6
3.	Bc4	Bc5
4.	d3	d6
5.	Nc3	Nf6
6.	Bg5	

This move of White's pins the Black Knight, which, if it moves away, leaves Black's Queen exposed to capture by the White Bishop. Black must play carefully at this juncture; suppose he is careless:

	White	Black
6.	. . .	0 – 0?
7.	Nd5	a6?
8.	B×f6	g×f6
9.	Qd2	f5
10.	Qh6	f6
11.	N×f6+	

An interesting situation has arisen with Black in double check (from White's Bishop and Knight). Therefore Black has to move his King – he cannot just capture the Knight with his Rook because that would leave his King still in check from White's Bishop.

	White	Black
11.	. . .	Kh8
12.	Q×h7 mate	

However, if Black plays carefully:

	White	Black
6.	. . .	h6

This move of Black's chases the White Bishop away. White can still maintain the pin by playing Bh4, which might tempt Black to launch a pawn attack on the King's side.

| 7. | Bh4 | g5 |

Beginners should also be warned about the **Vienna Gambit**:

1.	e4	e5
2.	Nc3	Nf6
3.	f4	

the best move for Black is d5, but it looks complicated, so beginners often play:

3.	. . .	e×f4?
4.	e5	Qe7?
5.	Qe2	

The Black Knight just has to return home to its starting square or worse may befall it:

5.	. . .	Ng8
6.	d4	d6
7.	Nd5	Qd8
8.	N×c7+	

if Black takes the Knight with his Queen, then e×d6+ wins the Queen.

VI

ENDING THE GAME

16. MATING WITH KING AND ROOK

Kings may not occupy adjoining squares so they become powerful pieces against each other in many endgame positions. If the problem is how to mate the Black King with just King and Rook, then driving the Black King into a corner is one answer. But, equally, once the Black King is confined to one of the files or ranks at the edge of the board by the White King standing before him, the Rook can mate the Black King on that file or rank.

Good chess players rarely take a game to an ending with only three or four pieces on the board; they give their opponents credit for being familiar with the stock ways of obtaining checkmate with various combinations of pieces, and so they resign at an earlier stage when their opponent has a decided advantage. A player who feels he is getting nowhere with his attack very often offers his opponent a draw, but his opponent need not accept – indeed, should not accept if he thinks he can see the game turning his way in a move or two. An offer of a draw is normally made verbally, but, when resigning, the customary way is to offer one's hand while toppling the King over on the board or, in jocular parlance, playing 'King to box'.

Some games end almost before they have begun. Fool's Mate is checkmate in just two moves as follows:

	White		*Black*	
1.	P – KB3	(b3)	P – K4	(e5)
2.	P – Kt4	(g4)	Q – KR5 mate	(Qh4+ +)

but such moves by White are not very likely!

But here is an opening much loved by many beginners because it is a way of defeating an unwary opponent in just four moves. It is called Scholar's Mate and consists of a concerted attack by White on Black's weakest pawn – the King's Bishop's pawn (f7), and weakest because it is the only pawn defended solely by the King and not by any other piece. It is worth playing out on the board to familiarise oneself with the threat:

57

17. FOOL'S MATE

Fool's Mate: White must indeed be a fool to play these moves and allow Black to checkmate him with the Queen in only the first two moves.

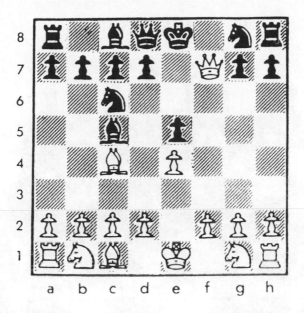

Danger – Scholar's Mate: a four-move disaster for Black.

Scholar's Mate

	White		Black	
1.	P – K4	(e4)	P – K4	(e5)
2.	B – QB4	(c4)	Kt – QB3	(c6)
3.	Q – KB3	(Qf3)	B – B4	(Bc5)
4.	Q × KBp	(mate) (Q×f7+ +)		

Black can easily avoid the immediate threat by playing
3 . . . Kt – KB3 (Nf6), but a more sophisticated attack on
the King's pawn (f7) by a White Knight and Bishop, with
back-up from other pieces, can make for an exciting game.
Black, of course, can make a similar attack on White's
pawn (KBp, f2).

59

18. SCHOLAR'S MATE

White to move: Scholar's Mate inevitable.

Scholar's Mate achieved.

Beginners sometimes behave like the original chess computers set at the lowest level, and to exchange pieces whenever the occasion arises. This may not be the best policy unless there is a particular reason for doing so. Certainly if a player is under pressure, and anxious to extricate himself from a tricky situation, exchanging pieces clears the board and can often diffuse an opponent's attack, particularly when it involves an exchange of Queens. But a player should try to ensure he is not down on any exchanges. However, if a player finds that he has gained a material advantage over his opponent as a result of a series of exchanges, it is probably wise policy for him to exchange as many other pieces as possible so that in the endgame his piece advantage can be fully exploited. Some games sometimes develop into a bit of carnage, and one side may be left with perhaps one or two pieces against the opposing King. It is desirable to know how to attain checkmate in this situation, and prevent the opponent achieving stalemate. Here are some of the combinations:

White	*Black*
1. King and Queen versus . . .	King.

This is an easy win for White provided care is taken and stalemate avoided. The Black King is chased to the side of the board by the White King and mated by the Queen standing in front of and protected by the White King.

2. King and Rook versus . . .	King.

A win for White by positioning the Rook to confine the Black King to two side files or ranks, and with the White King driving him towards a corner or hedging him in on the edge of the board.

3. King and two Bishops versus . . .	King.

A win for White, the Bishops can work in tandem and seal

off an area, confining the Black King to it while the White King drives the Black King into a corner.

4. King, Bishop and Knight versus . . . King.

A win for White, but harder for a beginner to execute.

5. King and Bishop or
    King and Knight or   }   versus King.
    King and two Knights

These are draws.

6. King and pawn versus . . .   King.

This is often a win for White because the White King tries to escort the pawn to the eighth rank and promote it to a Queen; but Black can sometimes make it a draw. Consider the following position:

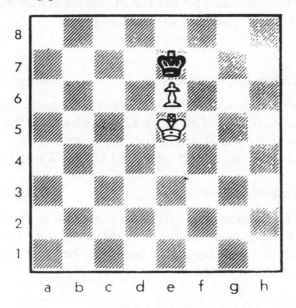

	White		*Black*	
1.	K – K5	(Ke5)	K – K1	(Ke8)
		see diagram		
2.	K – Q6	(Kd6)	K – Q1	(Kd8)
3.	P – K7ch	(e7+)	K – K1	(Ke8)
4.	K – K6	(ke6)		
		stalemate		

Any other move of the White King only results in the loss of the pawn and therefore a draw.

However, if White's King is in front of his pawn, the White King can drive the Black King out of the way, and escort the pawn till it reaches the eighth rank and becomes a Queen. After which victory for White is easy.

19. MATING WITH KING AND PAWN

By careful play Black can prevent this pawn queening, and can make the game a draw.

Pawn endings need to be played with great care to avoid being in Zugzwang (German for 'compulsion to move'). This occurs when a player has no spare moves left on the board – as when, for example, the battle has come to push of pawns and his are blocked against opposing pawns; in such a situation he is obliged to move his King, so permitting the opposing King to occupy a vital square.

The following nine-move game was played (and lost) by the great chess player Philidor, when he was a boy. It is worth playing through on a board to illustrate a number of features, including the pin of White's Knight by Black's Bishop on move 4 (if the White Knight moves, the Bishop takes the White Queen). It also shows how a line of pawns can support each other (Black shows this on move 2 and White shows this with move 6).

Notice also how White's King's Bishop is supporting the pawn, and in return is supported by it – a strong combination (move 6):

	White		*Black*	
1.	P – K4	(e4)	P – K4	(e5)
2.	B – B4	(Bc4)	P – Q3	(d6)
3.	Kt – KB3	(Nf3)	P – Kkt3	(g6)
4.	Kt – B3	(Nc3)	B – Kt5	(Bg4)
5.	P – KR3	(h3)	B – R4	(Bh5)
6.	P – Q3	(d3)	P – KR3	(h6)
7.	Kt × P	(N×e5)	B × Q	(B×d1)
8.	B × Pch	(B×f7+)	K – K2	(Ke7)
9.	Kt – Q5 mate	(Nd5++)		

It also shows how sometimes a bold attack (White's move 7, Kt×P) sacrificing the Queen, can turn out to produce an even greater prize – checkmate. Notice also that it is not always the best play to take an enemy piece offered (Black's B×Q on move 7, or the rejected K×B by White on move 9); on the chess board – as in life – there are

64

sometimes more important considerations than merely amassing material advantages.

One cannot easily cheat in chess because everything is literally above board. But there is scope for some games-manship – and worse. In championship matches forty moves have to be made inside two and a half hours, and this is done by each player pressing a button as he makes his move, which stops his own clock and starts that of his opponent; but in one match an Argentinian grandmaster was so incensed by the apparent slowness of his opponent's clock that he picked it up and ran off with it.

Usually, unsporting behaviour is less dramatic. Some players have irritating but perhaps unconscious habits and ticks (such as tapping with a finger, creaking their chair or grinding their teeth), which can play havoc with an opponent's concentration. In the match in which Karpov took the world title from Korchnoi, the accusations were not just of ticks but of actual kickings under the table. Sometimes behaviour is just prima donna-ish, as when Fischer in 1972 insisted on his favourite chair being flown from New York to Iceland for his match against Spassky, and then objected to the colour of the carpet in the tournament room because he felt it clashed with his green suit. In the same match Spassky insisted his chair be searched for electrical devices. However, in mitigation for such behaviour it should be said that in the atmosphere of intense concentration demanded by such cerebral confrontations, almost any detail can become a distraction, as, for instance, when Korchnoi complained, when he was playing in a match against Karpov, that a member of the audience was attempting hypnotism, while Karpov believed that another person in the audience was practising telepathy.

It is worth bearing in mind that there is no luck in chess as there is in card games, and, if one loses, it is one's own fault. A philosophical attitude is desirable so as not to mind losing too much, perhaps by keeping in mind the old saying that 'the chess winner is only the chap who made the last blunder but one'. The homely adage about putting every defeat down to experience is helpful, and comfort can be gleaned from George Bernard Shaw's remark to other indifferent players: 'Chess is a foolish expedient for making idle people believe they are doing something very clever'. Moreover, good chess players are not more likely than anyone else to be good people. Howard Staunton was undoubtedly the best chess player in the world in his day, but he seemed to resent anyone whose chess talent even approached his own; as an obituary in the *Hartford Times* on 26 September 1874, expressed it, he was 'too jealous of his fame and depreciated other players until the chess world failed to appreciate him.' The real dilemma of chess, as F. Mendelssohn pointed out, is that 'it is too earnest for a game and yet too much of a game to be earnest about'. However, really enthusiastic chess participants who take the game seriously – as contrasted with the great majority of chess players who confine themselves to what are called friendly games – can gain a British grading as a measure of their chess ability, and over 10,000 people in the United Kingdom are so listed. It is usual to enter a chess congress and play against graded opponents for a player's grade to be calculated. The British Chess Federation's Grading System is a measure of a player's strength of play, ranging from a beginner, who may have a grade of 40, to an international grandmaster with a grade in excess of 250. To qualify for grading games must, of course, be played with clocks, and a thirty move session must be played at an average speed no greater than two minutes per move. Points are given for each game, recorded as follows: the opponent's grade plus fifty points for each win; the opponent's grade alone for each draw; and the opponent's grade, minus fifty points for each loss – the opponent's grade being taken from the BCF grading lists. To avoid undue distortion, if the difference in grading between two players is more than 40, then it is assumed to be precisely

40 in the calculations. Players under the age of eighteen are presumed to be improving each year so their grade is increased by ten points. A player's grade is calculated by dividing the total number of points credited to him by the number of recorded games (at least 18) he has played – these calculations being carried out by volunteers who receive the results from the organisers of chess congresses and other events, and pass them to the British Chess Federation at 9a Grand Parade, St. Leonards-on-Sea, East Sussex.

Club players can be found with grades below 100 for a class D weakish player, to 174 for a strong club class A player, and up to 200 for a club or county champion. Congress winners and strong national players will often have grades between 200 and 224, with only British master players of international status rising above that.

In America the rating system was formulated by the American Professor Arpad Elo, and is based on a player's tournament results over a period. A player can normally qualify for an international rating from the World Chess Federation (FIDE) after nine games against players who already have FIDE ratings of better than 2200 Elo points, which is equal to 200 on the British grading system (to convert, multiply the British grade by 8 and add 600).

To qualify for a title in chess a player must perform well against master players. Current international titles are FIDE Master, for which qualification is 24 games at performance level 2351 (British equivalent grade is 219), International Master, level 2451 (British equivalent 231), and Grandmaster, level 2601 (British equivalent 250) – but there are only around two hundred Grandmasters in the whole world, nearly half of them from the USSR, where an international title qualifies a player for a State salary. The highest number of Elo points any player has ever attained up to 1989 was 2785 by Fischer of the USA. The current world champion Kasparov scored 2775 Elo points in the FIDE rating list for January 1989, with Karpov gaining

2750, and from the UK, Short 2650, Speelman 2640, Nunn 2620, Hodgson 2545, and Susan Arkell 2310. The Hungarian Judit Polgar – still only twelve years old in January 1989 – scored 2555. For historical reasons, women's titles are set at lower levels, but this is likely to change as women's chess performance comes to equal men's.

Grandmasters of chess often agree a draw at a stage when it may seem to beginners that there is a lot of steam still left in the game and many opportunities still to play for. The following position, reached in the 10th game of the World Chess Championship in Seville in November 1987, is a case in point. After Kasparov playing White had made his 20th move, he agreed a draw with Karpov. Each side had only lost four pieces, and lines of attack and defence may look promising, yet neither player wished to continue with what, upon examination, is an equally-balanced position.

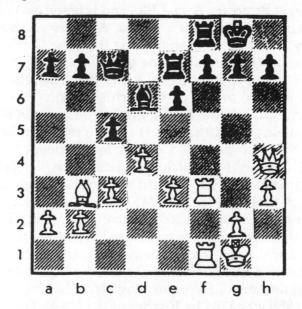

One useful point to notice about playing the endgame is that the result is often determined by which side has to

68

move. Consider the position where the Black King is on e7 and the White King on e5, then, if it is Black's turn, the White King is said to 'to have the opposition'. This is an advantage for White as it means that the Black King has to concede control of some squares when he moves. Similarly, the result of some games turns upon whether a pawn can reach promotion on the eighth rank before the enemy King can catch him. To obviate the need for arduous counting of squares, it is easy to calculate this by drawing an imaginary square on the board extending to the eighth rank with the pawn in one corner, if the opposing King is within the square then the pawn is doomed, but if the enemy King is outside and never penetrates the square, then promotion can take place before capture is possible.

20. SMOTHERED MATE?
An illustration of the occasional value of underpromotion

By the look of this position, Black has but to advance his pawn one square to the eighth rank, promote it to a Knight and the game is won. By this one move White is checkmated – the White King being smothered. But the position is obviously contrived – indeed, almost impossible – because, quite apart from the unbelievable jumble of the White pieces, the Black King is on h3, and there is hardly any way he is likely to have got there past White's f and g pawns.

Common ways of achieving checkmate in the endgame are illustrated in the following diagrams:

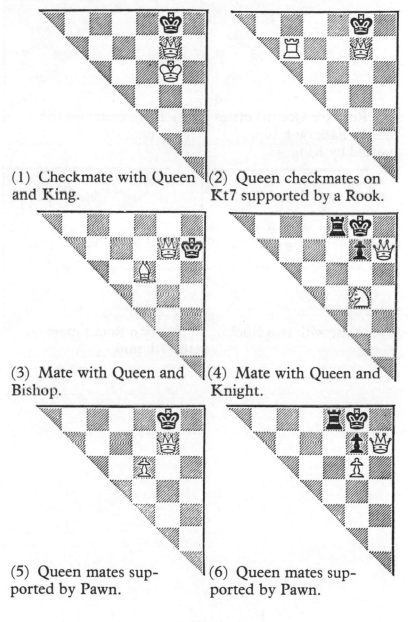

(1) Checkmate with Queen and King.

(2) Queen checkmates on Kt7 supported by a Rook.

(3) Mate with Queen and Bishop.

(4) Mate with Queen and Knight.

(5) Queen mates supported by Pawn.

(6) Queen mates supported by Pawn.

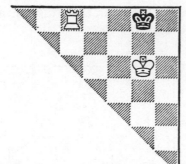

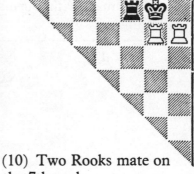

(7) Rook (or Queen) mates on the back rank supported by King.

(8) Rook mates on the back rank.

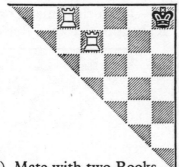

(9) Mate with two Rooks.

(10) Two Rooks mate on the 7th rank.

End-of-Book Test for Beginners

Question 1:

In the position in the diagram below, Black is to move: why can't Black afford to take the White Knight with his Queen?

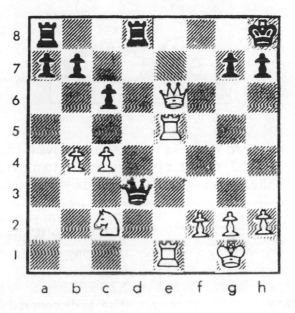

Answer:

Because if he does, White will achieve mate by:

1.	Qe8+	R×c8
2.	Re8+	R×e8
3.	Re8++	

Question 2:

White to play and mate in five moves.

Answer:

The danger to White in the position above is that Black will play Qh2++. But it is White's turn to move, and in fact White has a neat mate in five moves, as follows:

1.	Qd5+	Black cannot respond with Kf8 as White could then play Qf7++.
1.	. . .	Kh8
2.	Nf7+	Kg8
3.	Nh6+	This is discovered check from the White Queen, so Black cannot capture the Knight with the g pawn. Black cannot play Kf8 because Qf7 would be mate.
3.	. . .	Kh8
4.	Qg8+!	Now this is a sacrifice of the Queen, but to good purpose.
4.	. . .	R×g8
5.	Nf7++	

Question 3:

Why would it be a poor move for the White Queen to take the pawn in the position below?

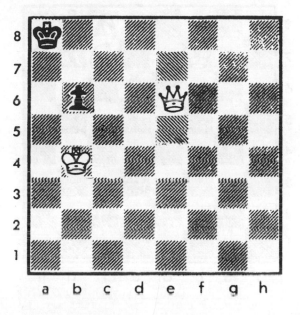

Answer:

If the White Queen takes the pawn on b6, then Black has no legitimate move left. The position is then stalemate and the result of the game a draw.

Question 4:

White to move and mate in one.

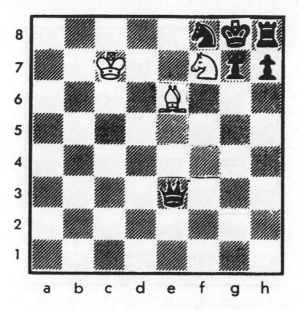

Answer:

Nh6 gives double check to Black's King. The Black
Queen can capture both the offending White Bishop
and the Knight – but not both in the same move – so
Black is mated.

Question 5:

White has no way of winning this unequal contest, but he can make it a draw. How?

Answer:

By playing Qf7+ followed by Qf8+ and then Qf7+ so as to obtain perpetual check, and so a draw.

Question 6:
White to move and mate in two moves.

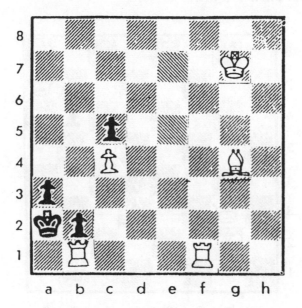

Answer:

This is a simple chess puzzle incorporating some useful lessons. Of course, White has such a material preponderance that the issue cannot be in doubt, provided Black does not rescue himself from his difficulties by achieving stalemate. Note that in the position above, Black has only one legitimate move he can make, and White must be very careful not to box Black in so that he is denied the win by a stalemate. The easiest way for White to win (and in two moves) is B – Q1 (Bd1) which blocks the previously-mentioned legitimate move (Kb3) and forces Black to take the offered Rook with his King. Then White can play B – QKt3 (Bb3) discovering check from the other Rook – which position is also mate.

Question 7:
How does White avoid defeat? (White to move.)

Black: Philip Berkovi

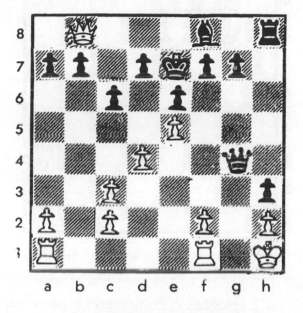

White: Jonathan Stanley

Answer:

It is 1.58 p.m. in this friendly game between pupils played at Bancroft's School on 23 January, 1978. Black is preparing to play Qf3 if White tries a defensive move such as Rg1. What can White do to stave off defeat before classes begin at 2 o'clock? The answer came easily; White played Qd6+ followed by Qb8+ followed again by Qd6+ thus giving perpetual check and forcing his frustrated opponent to a draw.

Question 8:

Who wins this game? (White to move.)

Answer:

Rules and Logic can sometimes seem to part company in chess. Who, for example, won the game above? White played Bg2+ and announced that he would have mate on the next move. Black disagreed and played d5+ thus not only interposing his pawn between the Bishop and the King but disclosing check on the White King, which is also indeed mate. White has in fact composed a neat sui – mate in one. But White objects saying that Black's d pawn never reached the 5th rank, but was taken by White's c pawn en passant on d6, and, since dead men cannot shoot, Black was already checkmated before his d pawn reached d5. In fact the rules give Black the win; but in logic there is something to be said for White's argument.

Question 9:

White plays Be3, which at first sight looks like a mistake but is actually a trap. Why should Black not respond by N×e3?

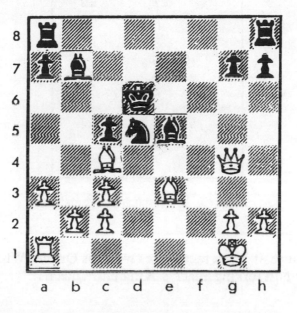

Answer:

Because White can then play Qe6+ which obliges the Black King to move to c7; after which White captures the Bishop by Q×c5+ followed by capture of the Knight (Q×e3).

Question 10:
Why may White safely take the Rook with his Queen?

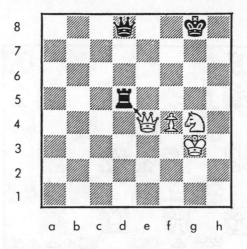

Answer:

Because, if Black recaptures with his Queen, White can play Nf6 forking Black's King and Queen.

Here is a neat little mate composed by a Frenchman, Kermur de Legal, in 1750, and demonstrating how sacrificing the Queen may well be worthwhile on rare occasions!

	White	*Black*
1.	e4	e5
2.	Nc3	Nc6
3.	f4	d6
4.	Nf3	e × f4
5.	Bc4	Ne5
6.	Bb3	Bg4
7.	N × e5	. . .

this moves leaves the White Queen en prise, a bait which Black mindlessly accepts

7.	. . .	B × d1
8.	B × f7 +	Ke7
9.	Nd5 + +	

Some chess terms explained

an active piece	–	a piece which is well positioned.
a combination	–	when two or more men work together to attack an opponent's piece.
a double attack	–	when two men attack one man.
doubled pawns	–	pawns of the same side in the same file.
a flight square	–	a square to which an attacked man may retreat.
a forced move	–	a move which is the only legal one available.

an illegal move	–	a move which breaks the rules.
en prise	–	a man is en prise when threatened with capture (usually when without the option of immediate recapture).
an open file	–	a file on which there are no pawns of either side.
an overworked piece	–	a piece which is defending two or more men at the same time.
a passive piece	–	a piece which is not performing a useful function in its current position.
a Knight fork	–	a double attack by a Knight on two of the opponent's men.
a pin	–	a piece is pinned when, if it moves, it exposes another piece of its own side to attack.
a pawn fork	–	a double attack by a pawn on two of the opponent's men.

VII

CHESS-RELATED GAMES

For relief from defeat – or just for alternative entertainment – there are a number of chess-related games which the beginner may like to sample. Here are a few:

1. *Simultaneous Chess*
   This is where an expert player takes on a number of other players all at the same time. He can spare only a few moments to consider his move at each board as he walks round.

2. *Quickplay Chess and Blitz*
   This is chess where very limited time is allowed to make the moves. It is good practice and can be great fun. Quickplay chess obliges each player to make all his moves within thirty minutes; Blitz is even faster — each player has five minutes to make all his moves in the game, which means that in some games the endplay is a hectic scramble – or worse. In a quick-play tournament in Spain in 1988, one player who was desperately short of time was disqualified for keeping his hand permanently pressed down on his clock button so that only his opponent's clock was running. The game is increasingly popular, but does give an advantage to players who can think especially quickly, play intuitively, and are, of course, overly familiar with the move sequences of standard openings.

3. *Blindfold Chess*
   In this game an expert player plays one or more sighted opponents blindfolded (or more usually sitting with his back to the sets). He is told the moves and has to memorise them and visualise the boards in his head.

Philidor used to give demonstrations of this at the Court of Versailles.

4. *Fox and Geese*
Seven-year-olds enjoy this chase by two foxes (knights) of eight geese (pawns) who are trying to reach the sanctuary of the eighth rank. It is Chess's attempt to simulate draughts.

5. *Computer Chess*
A more serious game is the solitary satisfaction of playing against a chess computer. In this game one's opponent never objects to a move being taken back, and is prepared to change sides when one is getting the worst of the conflict. The strength of a chess computer is said to lie in four things: its opening book – that is its pre-determined opening moves (up to perhaps ten) which have been programmed into the computer based on the findings of modern analysis; its lack of emotion – it plays doggedly at the same strength throughout; its speed of thought, number crunching through the options to find the best combination at every move; and its ability – and this is in the next generation of computers – to begin to devise original ideas rather than just apply basic principles. Although not arrived at by the same process as the human mind, such ideas can none the less emerge from possibilities considered at random. Playing a chess computer is a good way of learning the game, especially playing with ones that will suggest moves to assist a beginner.

6. *Three Dimensional Chess*
This is played on three levels, as if the normal game were not complicated enough. After all, two-dimensional chess already is, as Howard Staunton wrote in *The Chess Player's Handbook*, 'the most fascinating intellectual pastime which the wisdom of antiquity has

bequeathed to us'.

7. *Hexagonal Chess*
The newest chess variation to catch on, this game
employs the chess pieces on a six-sided board. Conceived
by Wladyslaw Ginski in 1937, the first World Hexagonal
Chess Championships took place at the Polish Cultural
Institute in London in 1987. There is also Tri-Chess
played by three players, each with nineteen pieces on a
hexagonal board. The complexities are mind boggling.

8. *Kriegspiel*
The best of the chess-related games is probably
Kriegspiel, which involves three chess sets, two players
and one umpire. The moves are exactly as in chess
except that players see only their own men and are not
told their opponent's moves; only the umpire's board
has the true position of both players.

The rules may be summarised as follows. The two
contestants sit back to back, each with a board in front
of him with both sets of men set up for the start.
However, once the game has begun, White, for
example, can only be certain of the positions of the
White men on the board in front of him; he may move
the Black men on his board where he thinks they may
be, but his moves are guesses. The accurate position of
both sides is on the umpire's board hidden from view
of both players between their backs.

At each turn the umpire announces: 'White has
moved' or 'Black has moved', and carefully records the
moves on the umpire's board, making sure also that no
illegal moves are taking place. A player attempting to
move a Bishop, for instance, down a diagonal which,
unknown to the player, is blocked by an opposing
piece, is told by the umpire: 'No, you may not move
there'. The player must then try to move the Bishop
elsewhere, and usually will alight upon the piece that

87

has blocked his passage and capture it. Attempting to move a man at all means that it must move somewhere, provided that there is a legal move it can make. Thus, a pawn that attempts to move forward and finds its path blocked must try taking to either side; indeed, when wishing to move a pawn forward, it may be prudent to try taking on the adjoining files first – just in case there is a juicy catch to be had there.

1. *What questions can a player ask?*
(a) 'Can I do this?' – indicating a particular move. This question can be asked an indefinite number of times with as many men as the player wishes, the umpire answering 'yes' or 'no', but if the umpire answers 'yes', then the attempted move must be made. However, once a player attempts to move a man, all possible moves with that man must be attempted until a legitimate one is found.

2. *What announcements does the umpire make?*
  (a) When a King is in check, he makes one of the following announcements:
      (i) The White (or Black) King is in check on the diagonal.
      (ii) The White (or Black) King is in check to a Knight.
      (iii)The White (or Black) King is in check on a file or a rank.
      If a King is double-checked, both the checks are announced. Discovered checks are also announced.
  (b) When a man is captured:
      All captures are announced as soon as they have taken place, but the referee does not disclose what man has been taken but only on what square the capture has taken place, e.g. 'White has moved and has taken a man on e4'.

88

(c)   When an illegal or impossible move is attempted –
such as a player trying to move the King on to a
square where he would be in check – the umpire
says: 'No, you can't do that move', but does not
give the reason – the player has to work that out
for himself.

3. *Hints for Play*
(1)   Keep a clear record of how many men one's
opponent possesses by always removing from the
board a likely man when a capture is announced.
(2)   When a man has been captured by the opponent,
always place a likely man of one's opponent on the
square. It may be possible then to recapture on
that square within a move or so.
(3)   Avoid moving an opponent's pawn out of its file
unless fairly certain that the pawn in question has
captured one of one's men. It sometimes becomes
important towards the end of the game to know
exactly which enemy pawn is trying to gain
promotion.
(4)   In Kriegspiel, as in chess, it is wise to avoid
moving quickly – sit on your hands if tempted to
do so; and play the game hard to gain most
pleasure from it, but not too seriously, lest it
degenerate into what Sir Walter Scott called
chess: 'a sad waste of brains'.

Kriegspiel involves three people, and is also fun
for others who just watch. Computers have not yet
evolved to play it, whereas with chess, once a
beginner has mastered the sort of matter covered
in this book, a chess computer can be the best of
teachers and an agreeable (and never moody)
companion. The most expensive are of grand-

master class and, as development proceeds, are likely to become almost unbeatable by human opponents; but a relatively inexpensive model, provided it possesses the facility of suggesting best moves to its opponents, is nearly all a learner will find needed for hours of instructive enjoyment.

Chess is a difficult game
to learn to play well;
but, as W. B. Yeats observed:
'There is a fascination in what is difficult.'
It is only the too difficult
which causes frustration.

Beginners are recommended to buy a chess computer to help them learn the game. These can be obtained from
The Chess Computer Specialists,
P.O. Box 759, Witchampton,
Wimborne, Dorset BH21 5YH,
telephone: 0258 840285,
who will also be pleased to advise on the most suitable models.
